# Hippocrene
# CHILDREN'S
# ILLUSTRATED
# NORWEGIAN
# DICTIONARY

## ENGLISH · NORWEGIAN
## NORWEGIAN · ENGLISH

Compiled by the Editors of Hippocrene Books

Proofreading and Norwegian language translation by Siri Ostensen

Interior illustrations by S. Grant (24, 81, 88); J. Gress (page 10, 21, 24, 37, 46, 54, 59, 65, 72, 75, 77);
K. Migliorelli (page 13, 14, 18, 19, 20, 21, 22, 25, 31, 32, 37, 39, 40, 46, 47, 66, 71, 75, 76, 82, 86, 87);
B. Swidzinska (page 9, 11, 12, 13, 14, 16, 23, 27, 28, 30, 32, 33, 35, 37, 38, 41, 42, 45, 46, 47, 48, 49, 50,
52, 53, 56, 57, 58, 59, 60, 61, 62, 63, 66, 68, 69, 70, 71, 72, 73, 75, 77, 78, 79, 83), N. Zhukov (page 8, 13,
14, 17, 18, 23, 27, 29, 33, 34, 39, 40, 41, 52, 64, 65, 71, 72, 73, 78, 84, 86, 88).

Design, prepress, and production: Graafiset International, Inc.

Copyright © 2002 by Hippocrene Books, Inc.

All rights reserved.

Cataloging-in-Publication Data available from the Library of Congress.

ISBN 0-7818-0887-1

Printed in Hong Kong.

For information, address:
Hippocrene Books, Inc.
171 Madison Avenue
New York, NY 10016

# INTRODUCTION

With their absorbent minds, infinite curiosities and excellent memories, children have enormous capacities to master many languages. All they need is exposure and encouragement.

The easiest way to learn a foreign language is to simulate the same natural method by which a child learns English. The natural technique is built on the concept that language is representational of concrete objects and ideas. The use of pictures and words are the natural way for children to begin to acquire a new language.

The concept of this Illustrated Dictionary is to allow children to build vocabulary and initial competency naturally. Looking at the pictorial content of the Dictionary and saying and matching the words in connection to the drawings gives children the opportunity to discover the foreign language and thus, a new way to communicate.

The drawings in the Dictionary are designed to capture children's imaginations and make the learning process interesting and entertaining, as children return to a word and picture repeatedly until they begin to recognize it.

*The beautiful images and clear presentation make this dictionary a wonderful tool for unlocking your child's multilingual potential.*

Deborah Dumont, M.A., M.Ed.,
**Child Psychologist and Educational Consultant**

# Norwegian Pronunciation

| Letter(s) | Pronunciation system used |
|---|---|
| a | **ah** like the a in English "art" |
| b | **b** as in English "bent" |
| c | **s** as in English "sick" |
| d | **d** as in English "day" |
| d | at end of a word usually silent |
| e | **e** as in English "leg" |
| e | **eh** like the e in English "legend" |
| f | **f** as in English "fine" |
| g | **g** as in English "girl" |
| g | **y** as in English "yet" |
| g | **ng** at the end of a word as the ng in English "ring" |
| h | **h** as in English "hard" |
| i | **i** like in English "ring" |
| i | **ee** as in English "green" |
| j | **y** as in English "yet" |
| k | **k** like in English "key" |
| l | **l** as in English "leg" |
| m | **m** as in English "man" |
| n | **n** as in English "no" |
| o | **o** as the o in English "pot" |
| o | **oh** as the o in English "corner" |
| o | **oo** as in English "stool" |
| p | **p** like in English "pet" |
| q | **q** as in English "quarter" |
| r | **r** as in English "rich" |
| s | **s** as in English "sun" |
| sj | **sh** like in English "shoe" |
| sk | **sh** like in English "shoe" |
| sk | **sk** like in English "skill" |
| t | **t** as in English "tea" |
| u | **uh** as ew in English "brew" |
| v | **v** as in English "very" |
| w | **v** as in English "very" |
| x | **x** like the x in "Texas" |
| y | **yeh** as in English "yellow" |
| æ | **ay** as ai in English "air" |
| ø | **oe** like the i in English "Sir" |
| å | **oh** as in English "forest" |

**airplane**      **(et) fly**
*(et) flyeh*

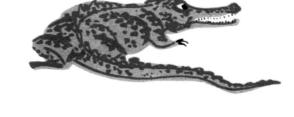

**alligator**      **(en) alligator**
**(ehn)** *ul-li-gah-tor*

**alphabet**      **(et) alfabet**
*(et) ul-fah-beht*

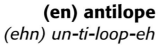

**antelope**      **(en) antilope**
*(ehn) un-ti-loop-eh*

**antlers**      **horn**
*hoorn*

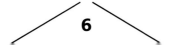

**apple** **(et) eple**
*(et) ep-leh*

**aquarium** **(et) akvarium**
*(et) uk-vah-ri-um*

**arch** **(en) bue**
*(ehn) buh-eh*

**arrow** **(en) pil**
*(ehn) peel*

**autumn** **(en) høst**
*(ehn) hoest*

**baby**      **(en) baby**
*(ehn) beh-bee*

**backpack**      **(en) ryggsekk**
*(ehn) ryehg-sekk*

**badger**      **(en) grevling**
*(ehn) grehv-ling*

**baker**      **(en) baker**
*(ehn) bah-kehr*

**ball**      **(en) ball**
*(ehn) bahl*

**balloon**      **(en) ballong**
*(ehn) bah-long*

**banana**　　**(en) banan**
*(ehn) bah-nahn*

**barley**　　**(et) byggkorn**
*(et) byehg-koorn*

**barrel**　　**(en) tønne**
*(ehn) toen-eh*

**basket**　　**(en) kurv**
*(ehn) kuhr-vh*

**bat**　　**(en) flaggermus**
*(ehn) flah-gehr-muhs*

**beach**　　**(en) badestrand**
*(ehn) bahd-eh-strun*

**bear** **(en) bjørn**
*(ehn) byoern*

**beaver** **(en) bever**
*(ehn) beh-ver*

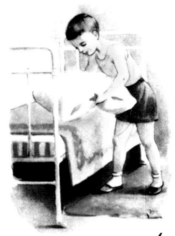

**bed** **(en/ei) seng**
*(ehn/ey) seng*

**bee** **(en) bie**
*(ehn) bee-eh*

**beetle** **(en) bille**
*(ehn) bil-leh*

**bell** **(en) bjelle**
*(ehn) byeh-leh*

**belt**　　　　　　　**(et) belte**
　　　　　　　　　　*(et) bel-teh*

**bench**　　　　　　**(en) benk**
　　　　　　　　　　*(ehn) benk*

**bicycle**　　　　　**(en) sykkel**
　　　　　　　　　　*(ehn) syeh-kehl*

**binoculars**　　　**(en) kikkert**
　　　　　　　　　　*(ehn) kyik-ehrt*

**bird**　　　　　　**(en) fugl**
　　　　　　　　　　*(ehn) fuh-lh*

**birdcage**　　　　**(et) fuglebur**
　　　　　　　　　　*(et) fuh-leh-buhr*

**black**      **svart**
*svahrt*

**blocks**      **klosser**
*kloh-sehr*

**blossom**      **(en) fruktblomst**
*(ehn) fruhkt-blohmst*

**blue**      **blå**
*bloh*

**boat**      **(en) båt**
*(ehn) boht*

**bone**      **(et) bein**
*(et) beyn*

**book** **(en) bok**
*(ehn) bohk*

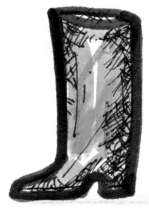

**boot** **(en) støvel**
*(ehn) stoe-vel*

**bottle** **(en) flaske**
*(ehn) fluss-keh*

**bowl** **(en) bolle**
*(ehn) bohl-leh*

**boy** **(en) gutt**
*(ehn) guht*

**bracelet** **(et) armbånd**
*(et) arm-bohn*

**branch**      **(en) grein**
*(ehn) grayn*

**bread**      **(et) brød**
*(et) broeh*

**breakfast**      **(en) frokost**
*(ehn) froo-kohst*

**bridge**      **(en) bro**
*(ehn) broo*

**broom**      **(en) kost**
*(ehn) kohst*

**brother**      **(en) bror**
*(ehn) broor*

**brown**           **brun**
*bruhn*

**brush**           **(en) børste**
*(ehn) boer-steh*

**bucket**           **(et) spann**
*(et) spun*

**bulletin board**      **(en) oppslagstavle**
*(ehn) op-slahgs-tahv-leh*

**bumblebee**           **(en) humle**
*(ehn) huhm-leh*

**butterfly**           **(en) sommerfugl**
*(ehn) sohm-mer-fuhl*

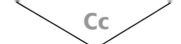

**cab**        **(en) drosje**
*(ehn) droh-sheh*

**cabbage**        **(et) kålhode**
*(et) kohl-hoh-deh*

**cactus**        **(en) kaktus**
*(ehn) kuk-tus*

**café**        **(en) kafé**
*(ehn) kah-feh*

**cake**        **(en) kake**
*(ehn) kah-keh*

**camel**        **(en) kamel**
*(ehn) kah-mehl*

**camera**　　　**(et) fotografiapparat**
*(et) foot-oo-grah-fee-ap-ar-aht*

**candle**　　　**(et) lys**
*(et) lyehs*

**candy**　　　**(et) sukkertøy**
*(et) soh-kehr-toey*

**canoe**　　　**(en) kano**
*(ehn) kah-noo*

**cap**　　　**(en/ei) lue**
*(ehn/ey) luh-eh*

**captain**　　　**(en) kaptein**
*(ehn) kahp-teyn*

**car** **(en) bil**
*(ehn) beel*

**card** **(et) kort**
*(et) kohrt*

**carpet** **(et) teppe**
*(et) tep-peh*

**carrot** **(en) gulrot**
*(ehn) guhl-root*

**(to) carry** **bære**
*bair-eh*

**castle** **(et) slott**
*(et) slot*

**cat** **(en) katt**
*(ehn) kut*

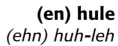

**cave** **(en) hule**
*(ehn) huh-leh*

**chair** **(en) stol**
*(ehn) stool*

**cheese** **(en) ost**
*(ehn) oost*

**cherry** **(et) kirsebær**
*(et) kyir-seh-bair*

**chimney** **(en/ei) pipe**
*(ehn/ey) pee-peh*

**chocolate**      **(en) sjokolade**
*(ehn) shook-oh-lah-deh*

**Christmas tree**      **(et) juletre**
*(et) yuh-leh-treh*

**circus**      **(et) sirkus**
*(et) sirr-kuhs*

**(to) climb**      **klatre**
*klah-treh*

**cloud**      **(en) sky**
*(ehn) shyeh*

**clown**      **(en) klovn**
*(ehn) klohvn*

**coach**      **(en) vogn**
*(ehn) vohgn*

**coat**      **(en) frakk**
*(ehn) fruk*

**coconut**      **(en) kokosnøtt**
*(ehn) koh-kohs-noet*

**comb**      **(en) kam**
*(ehn) kahmm*

**comforter**      **(en/ei) dyne**
*(ehn/ey) dyeh-neh*

**compass**      **(et) kompass**
*(et) kom-puss*

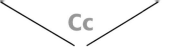

**(to) cook**  **lage mat**
*lah-geh maht*

**cork**  **(en) kork**
*(ehn) kohrk*

**corn**  **(en) maiskolbe**
*(ehn) mice-kohl-beh*

**cow**  **(en/ei) ku**
*(ehn/ey) kuh*

**cracker**  **(en) kjeks**
*(ehn) kyex*

**cradle**  **(en) vugge**
*(ehn) vuh-geh*

**(to) crawl**        **krabbe**
*kru-beh*

**(to) cross**        **gå over (gata)**
*goh ohv-er ga-tah*

**crown**        **(en) krone**
*(ehn) kroo-neh*

**(to) cry**        **gråte**
*groh-teh*

**cucumber**        **(en) agurk**
*(ehn) ah-gurk*

**curtain**        **(en) gardin**
*(ehn) gar-deen*

**(to) dance** **danse**
*(dun-seh)*

**dandelion** **(en) løvetann**
*(ehn) loeh-veh-tun*

**date** **(en) dato**
*(ehn) dah-too*

**deer** **(et) rådyr**
*(et) roh-dyehr*

**desert** **(en) ørken**
*(ehn) oer-ken*

**desk** **(en) pult**
*(ehn) puhlt*

**dirty** **skitten**
*shit-ehn*

**dog**       **(en) hund**
*(ehn) huhn*

**doghouse**      **(et) hundehus**
*(et) huhn-eh-huhs*

**doll**       **(en) dukke**
*(ehn) duh-keh*

**dollhouse**      **(et) dukkehus**
*(et) duh-keh-huhs*

**dolphin**      **(en) delfin**
*(ehn) del-feen*

**donkey**      **(et) esel**
*(et) eh-sel*

**dragon**      **(en) drage**
*(ehn) drah-geh*

**dragonfly** **(en) øyenstikker**
*(ehn) oey-ehn-stik-kehr*

**(to) draw** **tegne**
*tey-neh*

**dress** **(en) kjole**
*(ehn) kyool-eh*

**(to) drink** **drikke**
*drik-keh*

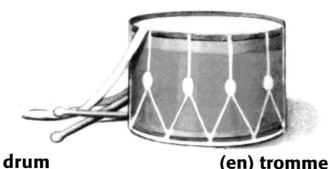

**drum** **(en) tromme**
*(ehn) trohm-meh*

**duck** **(en) and**
*(ehn) un*

**eagle**     **(en) ørn**
*(ehn) oern*

**(to) eat**     **spise**
*spee-seh*

**egg**     **(et) egg**
*(et) egg*

**eggplant**     **(en) eggplante**
*(ehn) egg-plahn-teh*

**eight**     **åtte**
*oht-eh*

**elbow**     **(en) albue**
*(ehn) al-buh-eh*

**elephant**     **(en) elefant**
*(ehn) e-le-funt*

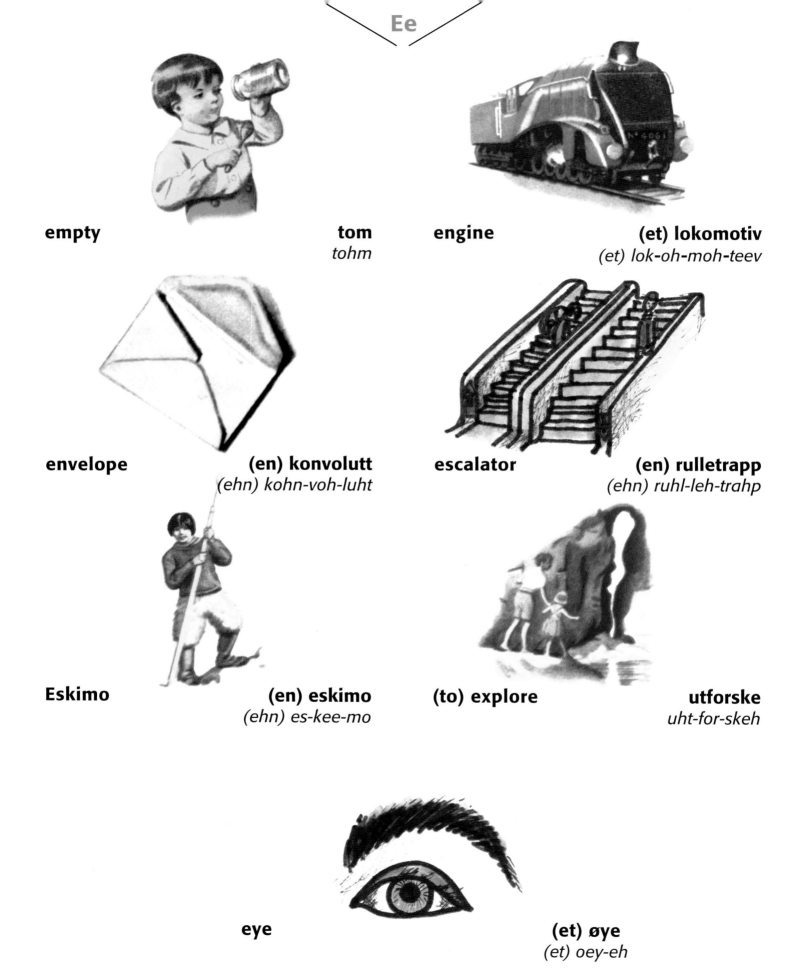

empty      **tom**
*tohm*

engine      **(et) lokomotiv**
*(et) lok-oh-moh-teev*

envelope      **(en) konvolutt**
*(ehn) kohn-voh-luht*

escalator      **(en) rulletrapp**
*(ehn) ruhl-leh-trahp*

**Eskimo**      **(en) eskimo**
*(ehn) es-kee-mo*

**(to) explore**      **utforske**
*uht-for-skeh*

eye      **(et) øye**
*(et) oey-eh*

**face** **(et) ansikt**
*(et) ahn-sikt*

**fan** **(en) vifte**
*(ehn) vif-teh*

**father** **(en) far**
*(ehn) fahr*

**fear** **(en) redsel**
*(ehn) red-sel*

**feather** **(en) fjær**
*(ehn) fyair*

**(to) feed** **mate**
*mah-teh*

**fence** **(et) gjerde**
*(et) yair-eh*

**fern** **(en) bregne**
*(ehn) bray-neh*

**field** **(et) jorde**
*(et) yoor-eh*

**field mouse** **(en/ei) markmus**
*(ehn/ey) mark-muhs*

**finger** **(en) finger**
*(ehn) fing-er*

**fir tree** **(et) grantre**
*(et) grahn-treh*

**fire**     **(et) bål**
*(et) bohl*

**fish**     **(en) fisk**
*(ehn) fisk*

**(to) fish**     **fiske**
*fiss-keh*

**fist**     **(en) knyttneve**
*(ehn) ke-nyeht-neh-veh*

**five**     **fem**
*fem*

**flag**     **(et) flagg**
*(et) flahg*

**flashlight**  **(en) lommelykt**
*(ehn) lohm-meh-lyehkt*

**(to) float**  **flyte**
*flyeh-teh*

**flower**  **(en) blomst**
*(ehn) blohmst*

**(to) fly**  **fly**
*flyeh*

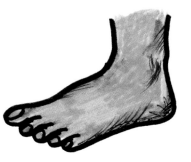

**foot**  **(en) fot**
*(ehn) foot*

**fork**  **(en) gaffel**
*(ehn) guf-fel*

**fountain**  **(et) springvann**
*(et) spring-vahn*

**four**      **fire**      **fox**      **(en) rev**
*feer-eh*      *(ehn) revh*

**frame**      **(en) ramme**
*(ehn) rahm-meh*

**friend**      **(en) venn**      **frog**      **(en) frosk**
*(ehn) vehn*      *(ehn) frohsk*

**fruit**      **(en) frukt**      **furniture**      **møbler**
*(ehn) fruhkt*      *moeb-ler*

**garden**          **(en) hage**
*(ehn) hah-geh*

**gate**          **(en) port**
*(ehn) poort*

**(to) gather**          **plukke**
*plohk-keh*

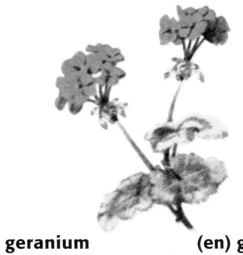

**geranium**          **(en) geranium**
*(ehn) geh-rah-nee-uhm*

**giraffe**          **(en) sjiraff**
*(ehn) shee-rahf*

**girl**          **(en/ei) jente**
*(ehn/ey) yent-eh*

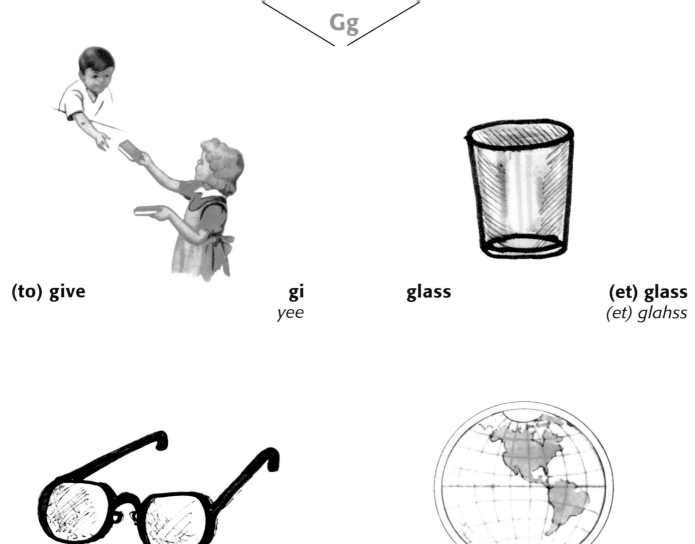

**(to) give**                    **gi**
                                 *yee*

**glass**                    **(et) glass**
                             *(et) glahss*

**glasses**                    **briller**
                               *bril-lehr*

**globe**                    **(en) globus**
                             *(ehn) gloo-buhs*

**glove**                    **(en) hanske**
                             *(ehn) hahn-skeh*

**goat**                    **(en/ei) geit**
                            *(ehn/ey) yeyht*

**goldfish**     **(en) gullfisk**
*(ehn) guhl-fisk*

**"Good Night"**     **"God natt"**
*goo-nut*

**"Good-bye"**     **"Adjø"**
*ad-yoe*

**goose**     **(en/ei) gås**
*(ehn/ey) gohs*

**grandfather**     **(en) bestefar**
*(ehn) bes-teh-fahr*

**grandmother**     **(en/ei) bestemor**
*(ehn/ey) bes-teh-mohr*

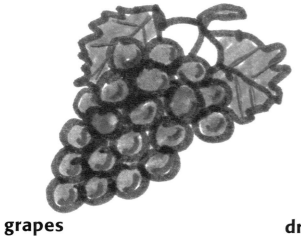

**grapes**　　　　　　　　**druer**
*druh-er*

**grasshopper**　　　**(en) gresshoppe**
*(ehn) grehs-hoh-peh*

**green**　　　　　　　　**grønn**
*groen*

**greenhouse**　　　**(et) drivhus**
*(et) dreev-huhs*

**guitar**　　　　　　　**(en) gitar**
*(ehn) gee-tahr*

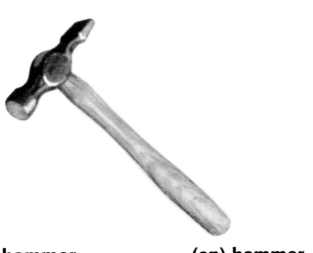

**hammer**     **(en) hammer**
*(ehn) hum-mer*

**hammock**     **(en) hengekøye**
*(ehn) heng-eh-koeyeh-eh*

**hamster**     **(et) hamster**
*(et) hum-ster*

**hand**     **(en) hånd**
*(ehn) hohn*

**handbag**     **(en) håndveske**
*(ehn) hohn-ves-keh*

**handkerchief**     **(et) lommetørkle**
*(et) lohm-meh-toerk-leh*

**harvest**     **(en) innhøsting**
*(ehn) in-hoest-ing*

**hat**     **(en) hatt**
*(ehn) hut*

**hay**     **(et) høy**
*(et) hoeyeh*

**headdress**     **(et) hodeplagg**
*(et) hoh-deh-plagh*

**heart**     **(et) hjerte**
*(et) yehr-teh*

**hedgehog**     **(et) pinnsvin**
*(et) pin-sveen*

**hen**      **(en/ei) høne**
*(ehn/ey) hoe-neh*

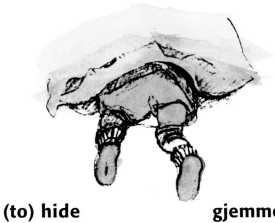

**(to) hide**      **gjemme seg**
*yehm-meh say*

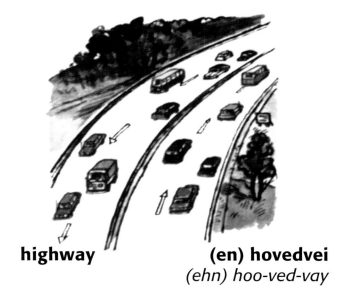

**highway**      **(en) hovedvei**
*(ehn) hoo-ved-vay*

**honey**      **(en) honning**
*(ehn) hoh-ning*

**horns**      **horn**
*hoorn*

**horse**      **(en) hest**
*(ehn) hest*

**horseshoe**

**(en) hestesko**
*(ehn) hest-eh-skoo*

**hourglass**

**(et) timeglass**
*(et) tee-meh-glahss*

**house**

**(et) hus**
*(et) huhs*

**(to) hug**

**klemme**
*kleh-meh*

**hydrant**

**(en) brannhydrant**
*(ehn) brun-hyeh-drant*

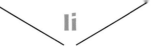

**ice cream**　　　**(en) iskrem**
*(ehn) ees-krehm*

**ice cubes**　　　**(en) isbit**
*(ehn) ees-beet*

**ice-skating**　　　**(et) skøyteløp**
*(et) shoeyeh-teh-loep*

**instrument**　　　**(et) instrument**
*(et) in-struh-ment*

**iris**　　　**(en) iris**
*(ehn) ee-ris*

**iron**　　　**(et) strykejern**
*(et) stryeh-keh-yehrn*

**island**　　　**(en/ei) øy**
*(ehn/ey) oey*

**jacket** **(en) jakke**
*(ehn) yak-keh*

**jam** **(et) syltetøy**
*(et) syehl-teh-toey*

**jigsaw puzzle** **(et) puslespill**
*(et) puhs-leh-spil*

**jockey** **(en) jockey**
*(ehn) yok-kee*

**juggler** **(en) sjonglør**
*(ehn) shohng-loer*

**(to) jump** **hoppe**
*hohp-eh*

**kangaroo**      **(en) kenguru**
*(ehn) keng-guh-ruh*

**key**      **(en) nøkkel**
*(ehn) noek-ehl*

**kitten**      **(en) kattunge**
*(ehn) kut-uhng-eh*

**knife**      **(en) kniv**
*(ehn) ke-neev*

**knight**      **(en) ridder**
*(ehn) rid-dehr*

**(to) knit**      **strikke**
*strik-keh*

**knot**      **(en) knute**
*(ehn) ke-nuht-eh*

**koala bear**      **(en) koalabjørn**
*(ehn) koh-ah-lah-byoern*

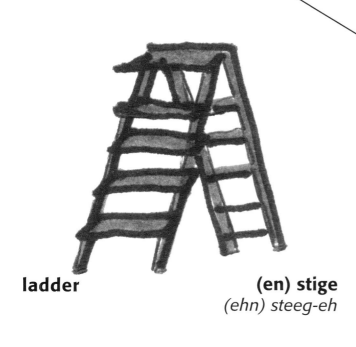

**ladder**  **(en) stige**
*(ehn) steeg-eh*

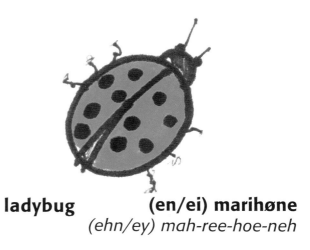

**ladybug**  **(en/ei) marihøne**
*(ehn/ey) mah-ree-hoe-neh*

**lamb**  **(et) lam**
*(et) lahmm*

**lamp**  **(en) lampe**
*(ehn) lahm-peh*

**(to) lap**  **slikke i seg**
*slik-keh ee say*

**laughter**  **(en) latter**
*(ehn) laht-tehr*

**lavender**　　　　　**(en) lavendel**
*(ehn) lah-ven-del*

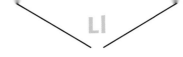

**lawn mower**　　　**(en) gressklipper**
*(ehn) grehss-klip-pehr*

**leaf**　　　　　　　**(et) blad**
*(et) blah*

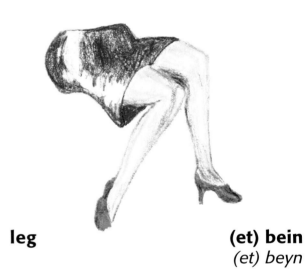

**leg**　　　　　　　　**(et) bein**
*(et) beyn*

**lemon**　　　　　　**(en) sitron**
*(ehn) sit-roon*

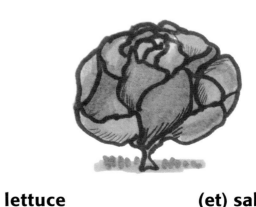

**lettuce**　　　　　　**(et) salathode**
*(et) sah-laht-hoh-deh*

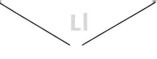

**lightbulb**     **(en) lyspære**
*(ehn) lyehs-peyr-eh*

**lighthouse**     **(et) fyr**
*(et) fyehr*

**lilac**     **(en) syren**
*(ehn) syeh-rehn*

**lion**     **(en) løve**
*(ehn) loe-veh*

**(to) listen**     **lytte**
*lyeht-teh*

**lobster**     **(en) hummer**
*(ehn) hohm-mehr*

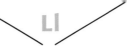

**lock**          **(en) lås**
*(ehn) lohs*

**lovebird**         **(en) turteldue**
*(ehn) tuhr-tel-duh-eh*

**luggage**        **bagasje**
*bug-ah-sheh*

**lumberjack**     **(en) tømmerhogger**
*(ehn) toem-mehr-hohg-gehr*

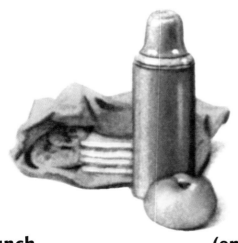

**lunch**          **(en) lunsj**
*(ehn) loensh*

**lynx**           **(en) gaupe**
*(ehn) geuh-peh*

Ll

48

**magazine**  **(et) ukeblad**
*(et) uhke-blah*

**magician**  **(en) tryllekunstner**
*(ehn) tryeh-leh-kuhnst-nehr*

**magnet**  **(en) magnet**
*(ehn) mug-neht*

**map**  **(et) kart**
*(et) kahrt*

**maple leaf**  **(et) lønneblad**
*(et) loen-neh-blah*

**marketplace**  **(et) torg**
*(et) tohrg*

**mask**  **(en) maske**
*(ehn) mus-keh*

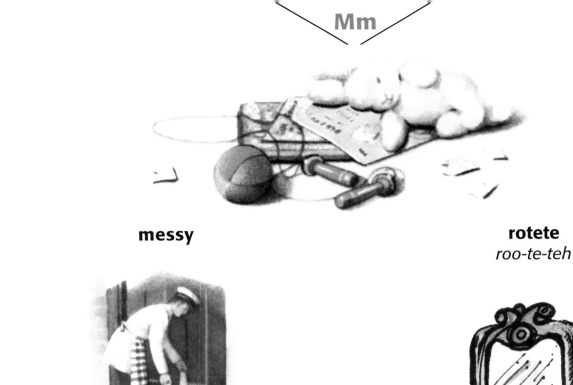

**messy**  **rotete**
*roo-te-teh*

**milkman**  **(en) melkemann**
*(ehn) mel-keh-mahnn*

**mirror**  **(et) speil**
*(et) speyl*

**mitten**  **(en) vott**
*(ehn) vohtt*

**money**  **penger**
*peng-ehr*

**monkey**  **(en) apekatt**
*(ehn) ah-pe-kut*

**moon**  **(en) måne**
*(ehn) moh-neh*

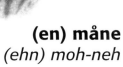

**mother**        **(en/ei) mor**
*(ehn/ey) moor*

**mountain**        **(et) fjell**
*(et) fyehll*

**mouse**        **(en/ei) mus**
*(ehn/ey) muhs*

**mouth**        **(en) munn**
*(ehn) muhn*

**mushroom**        **(en) sopp**
*(ehn) sohp*

**music**        **(en) musikk**
*(ehn) muh-sik*

**naked**     **naken**
*nah-ken*

**necklace**     **(et) halsbånd**
*(et) huls-bohnn*

**needle**     **(en/ei) nål**
*(ehn/ey) nohl*

**nest**     **(et) fuglerede**
*(et) fuh-leh-reh-deh*

**newspaper**     **(en) avis**
*(ehn) ah-vees*

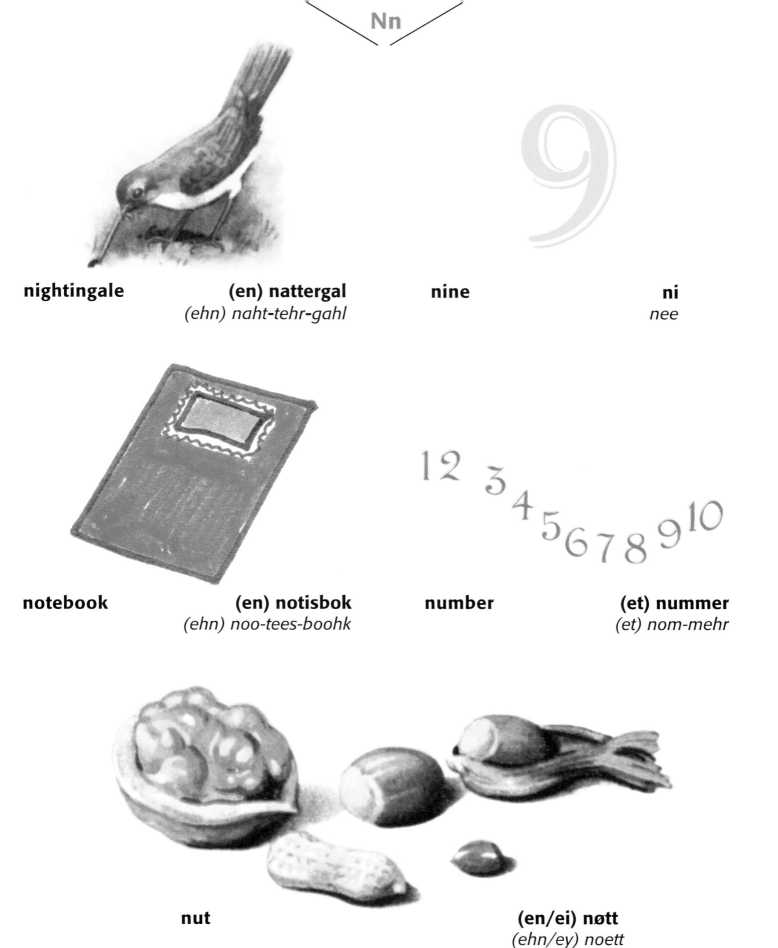

**nightingale**   **(en) nattergal**
*(ehn) naht-tehr-gahl*

**nine**   **ni**
*nee*

**notebook**   **(en) notisbok**
*(ehn) noo-tees-boohk*

**number**   **(et) nummer**
*(et) nom-mehr*

**nut**   **(en/ei) nøtt**
*(ehn/ey) noett*

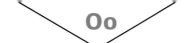

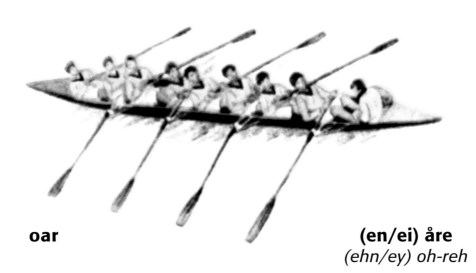

**oar**      **(en/ei) åre**
*(ehn/ey) oh-reh*

**ocean liner**      **(en) passasjerbåt**
*(ehn) pah-sah-shyehr-boht*

**old**      **gammel**
*gum-mehl*

**one**      **en/ei/et**
*(ehn/ey/et)*

**onion**      **(en) løk**
*(ehn) loehk*

**open**  **åpen**
*oh-pen*

**orange**  **(en) appelsin**
*(ehn) up-pel-seen*

**ostrich**  **(en) struts**
*(ehn) struhts*

**owl**  **(en) ugle**
*(ehn) uhg-leh*

**ox**  **(en) okse**
*(ehn) oks-eh*

**padlock** **(en) hengelås**
*(ehn) heng-eh-lohs*

**paint** **(en) farge**
*(ehn) fahr-geh*

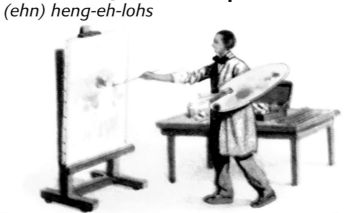

**painter** **(en) maler**
*(ehn) mah-lehr*

**pajamas** **(en) pyjamas**
*(ehn) pyeh-shah-mas*

**palm tree** **(et) palmetre**
*(et) pul-meh-treh*

**paper** **(et) papir**
*(et) pup-eer*

**parachute** **(en) fallskjerm**
*(ehn) fahll-shehrm*

**park**

**(en) park**
*(ehn) pahrk*

**parrot**

**(en) papegøye**
*(ehn) pah-peh-goey-eh*

**passport**

**(et) pass**
*(et) puss*

**patch**

**(en) lapp**
*(ehn) lahpp*

**path**

**(en) sti**
*(ehn) stee*

**peach**

**(en) fersken**
*(ehn) fayr-skehn*

**pear**

**(en) pære**
*(ehn) pay-reh*

**pebble** **(en) småstein**
*(ehn) smoh-steyn*

**(to) peck** **hakke**
*hahk-keh*

**(to) peel** **skrelle**
*skreh-leh*

**pelican** **(en) pelikan**
*(ehn) pe-lee-kan*

**pencil** **(en) blyant**
*(ehn) blyeh-ahnt*

**penguin** **(en) pingvin**
*(ehn) ping-veen*

**people** **(et) folk**
*(et) fohlk*

**piano**  **(et) piano**
*(et) pi-a-noo*

**pickle**  **(en) sylteagurk**
*(ehn) syeht-eh-ah-guhrk*

**pie**  **(en) pai**
*(ehn) pie*

**pig**  **(en) gris**
*(ehn) grees*

**pigeon**  **(en) due**
*(ehn) duh-eh*

**pillow**  **(en/ei) pute**
*(ehn/ey) puh-teh*

**pin**  **(en/ei) knappenål**
*(ehn/ey) ke-nahp-eh-nohl*

**pine** **(et) furutre**
*(et) fuh-ruh-treh*

**pineapple** **(en) ananas**
*(ehn) ah-nah-nahs*

**pit** **(en) kjerne**
*(ehn) kyehayr-neh*

**pitcher** **(en) mugge**
*(ehn) muhg-eh*

**plate** **(en) tallerken**
*(ehn) tah-lehrk-ehn*

**platypus** **(et) nebbdyr**
*(et) neb-dyehr*

**(to) play**　　　　**leke**
*leh-keh*

**plum**　　　　**(en) plomme**
*(ehn) plom-meh*

**polar bear**　　　　**(en) isbjørn**
*(ehn) ees-byoern*

**pony**　　　　**(en) ponni**
*(ehn) pon-nee*

**pot**　　　　**(en/ei) gryte**
*(ehn/ey) gryeh-teh*

**potato**　　　　**(en) potet**
*(ehn) poo-teht*

**(to) pour**        **skjenke**
*shehn-keh*

**present**        **(en) gave**
*(ehn) gah-veh*

**(to) pull**        **dra**
*drah*

**pumpkin**        **(et) gresskar**
*(et) gress-kahr*

**puppy**        **(en) valp**
*(ehn) vahlp*

**queen**        **(en/ei) dronning**
*(ehn/ey) drohn-ing*

**rabbit**

**(en) kanin**
*(ehn) kah-neen*

**raccoon**

**(en) vaskebjørn**
*(ehn) vahs-keh-byoern*

**racket**

**(en) tennisracket**
*(ehn) ten-nis-rehk-ket*

**radio**

**(en) radio**
*(ehn) rah-di-oo*

**radish**

**(en) reddik**
*(ehn) reh-dik*

**raft**  **(en) gummibåt**
*(ehn) guh-mih-boht*

**rain**  **(et) regn**
*(et) reyn*

**rainbow**  **(en) regnbue**
*(ehn) reyn-buh-eh*

**raincoat**  **(en) regnfrakk**
*(ehn) reyn-frahk*

**raspberry**  **(et) bringebær**
*(et) bring-eh-bayr*

**(to) read**          **lese**
*leh-seh*

 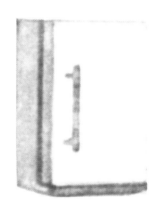

**red**      **rød**      **refrigerator**      **(et) kjøleskap**
        *roeh*             *(et) kyoe-leh-skahp*

**rhinoceros**      **(et) nesehorn**      **ring**      **(en) ring**
        *(et) neh-seh-hoorn*           *(ehn) ring*

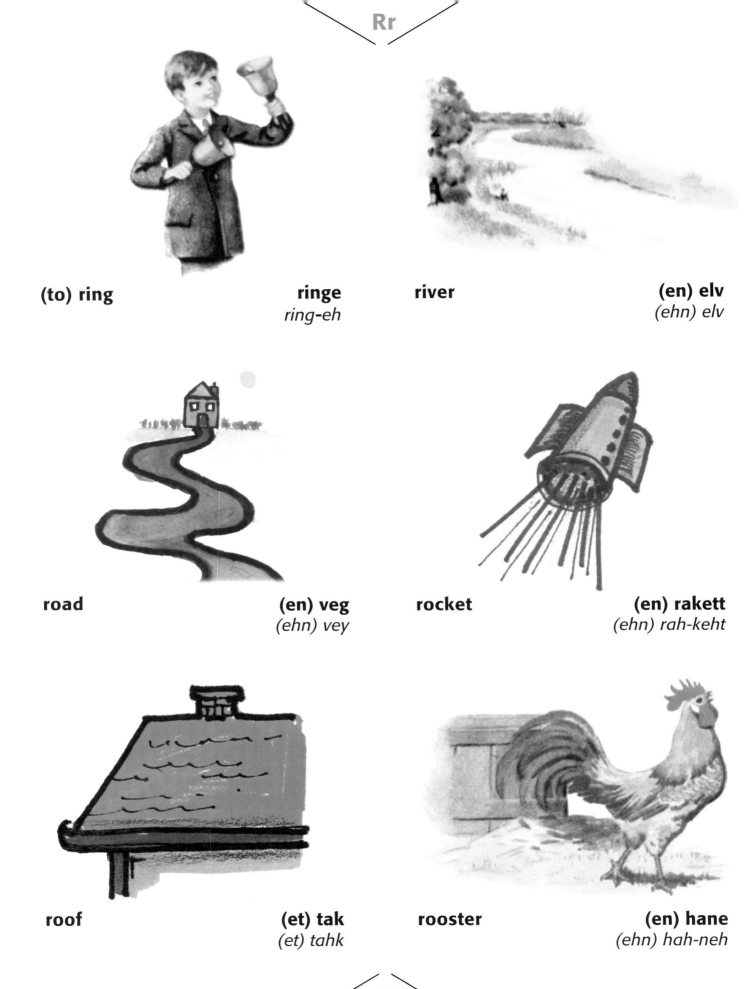

**(to) ring**    **ringe**
*ring-eh*

**river**    **(en) elv**
*(ehn) elv*

**road**    **(en) veg**
*(ehn) vey*

**rocket**    **(en) rakett**
*(ehn) rah-keht*

**roof**    **(et) tak**
*(et) tahk*

**rooster**    **(en) hane**
*(ehn) hah-neh*

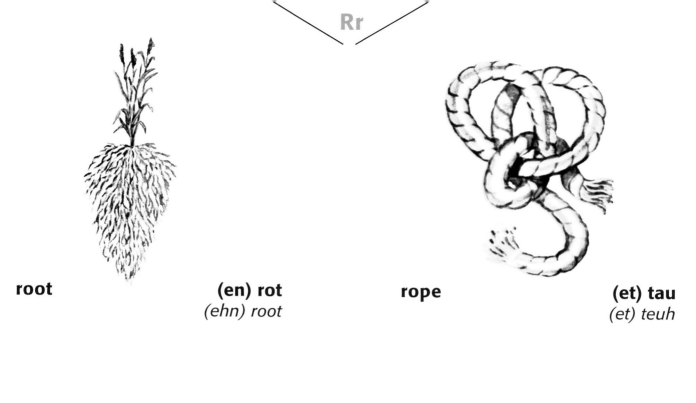

**root**     **(en) rot**
*(ehn) root*

**rope**     **(et) tau**
*(et) teuh*

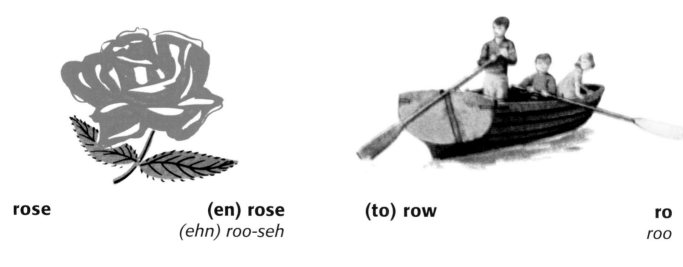

**rose**     **(en) rose**
*(ehn) roo-seh*

**(to) row**     **ro**
*roo*

**ruler**     **(en) linjal**
*(ehn) lin-yahl*

**(to) run**     **løpe**
*loe-peh*

**safety pin    (en/ei) sikkerhetsnål**
*(ehn/ey) sikh-ker-hehts-nohl*

**(to) sail                     seile**
*say-leh*

**sailor              (en) sjømann**
*(ehn) shoeh-mahn*

**salt                    (et) salt**
*(et) sahlt*

**scarf              (et) skjerf**
*(et) shehrf*

**school                  (en) skole**
*(ehn) skoo-leh*

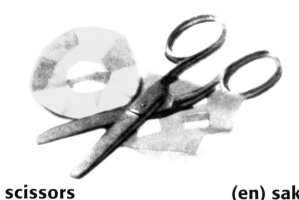

**scissors** **(en) saks**
*(ehn) sahx*

**screwdriver** **(et) skrujern**
*(et) skruh-jayrn*

**seagull** **(en) måke**
*(ehn) moh-keh*

**seesaw** **(en) dumphuske**
*(ehn) duhmp-huhs-keh*

**seven** **sju**
*shuh*

**(to) sew** **sy**
*syeh*

**shark**  **(en) hai**
*(ehn) hi*

**sheep**  **(en) sau**
*(ehn) seu*

**shell**  **(et) skjell**
*(et) shell*

**shepherd**  **(en) gjeter**
*(ehn) yeh-ter*

**ship**  **(et) skip**
*(et) sheep*

**shirt**  **(en) skjorte**
*(ehn) shoor-teh*

**shoe**        **(en) sko**
*(ehn) skoo*

**shovel**        **(en) spade**
*(ehn) spah-deh*

**(to) show**        **vise**
*vee-seh*

**shower**        **(en) dusj**
*(ehn) duhsh*

**shutter**        **(en) vindusskodde**
*(ehn) vin-duhs-skohd-deh*

**sick**        **sjuk**
*shuhk*

**sieve**

**(en) sil**
*(ehn) seel*

**(to) sing**

**synge**
*syehng-eh*

**(to) sit**

**sitte**
*sit-teh*

**six**

**seks**
*sex*

**sled**

**(en) kjelke**
*(ehn) ke-yelk-eh*

**(to) sleep**

**sove**
*soh-veh*

**small**   **liten**
*lee-ten*

**smile**   **(et) smil**
*(et) smeel*

**snail**   **(en) snegle**
*(ehn) sney-leh*

**snake**   **(en) slange**
*(ehn) slahng-eh*

**snow**   **(en) snø**
*(ehn) snoe*

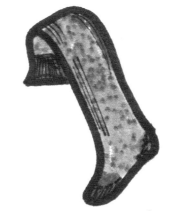

**sock**   **(en) strømpe**
*(ehn) stroem-peh*

**sofa**      **(en) sofa**
*(ehn) sof-fah*

**sparrow**      **(en) spurv**
*(ehn) spuhrv*

**spider**      **(en) edderkopp**
*(ehn) ed-der-kohp*

**spiderweb**      **(en) spindelvev**
*(ehn) spin-del-vehv*

**spoon**      **(en) skje**
*(ehn) sheh*

**squirrel**      **(et) ekorn**
*(et) ek-hohrn*

**stairs**      **(en) trapp**
*(ehn) trahp*

**stamp**      **(et) frimerke**
*(et) free-mayr-keh*

**starfish**      **(en) sjøstjerne**
*(ehn) shoe-styer-neh*

**stork**      **(en) stork**
*(ehn) stohrk*

**stove**      **(en) komfyr**
*(ehn) kom-fyehr*

**strawberry**      **(et) jordbær**
*(eht) yoor-bayr*

**subway**

**(en) tunnelbane**
*(ehn) tuh-nel-bah-neh*

**sugar cube**

**(en) sukkerbit**
*(ehn) sohk-ker-beet*

**sun**

**(en/ei) sol**
*(ehn/ey) sohl*

**sunflower**

**(en) solsikke**
*(ehn) sohl-sikk-eh*

**sweater**

**(en) genser**
*(ehn) gehn-ser*

**(to) sweep**

**feie**
*fey-eh*

**swing**

**(en) huske**
*(ehn) huhs-keh*

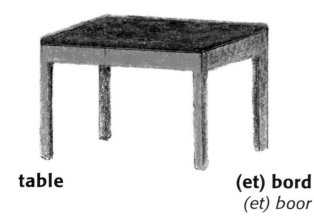

**table**        **(et) bord**
*(et) boor*

**teapot**        **(en) tekanne**
*(ehn) teh-kahn-eh*

**teddy bear**        **(en) teddybjørn**
*(ehn) ted-dee-byoern*

**television**        **(et) fjernsyn**
*(et) fyern-syehn*

10

**ten**        **ti**
*tee*

**tent**        **(et) telt**
*(et) telt*

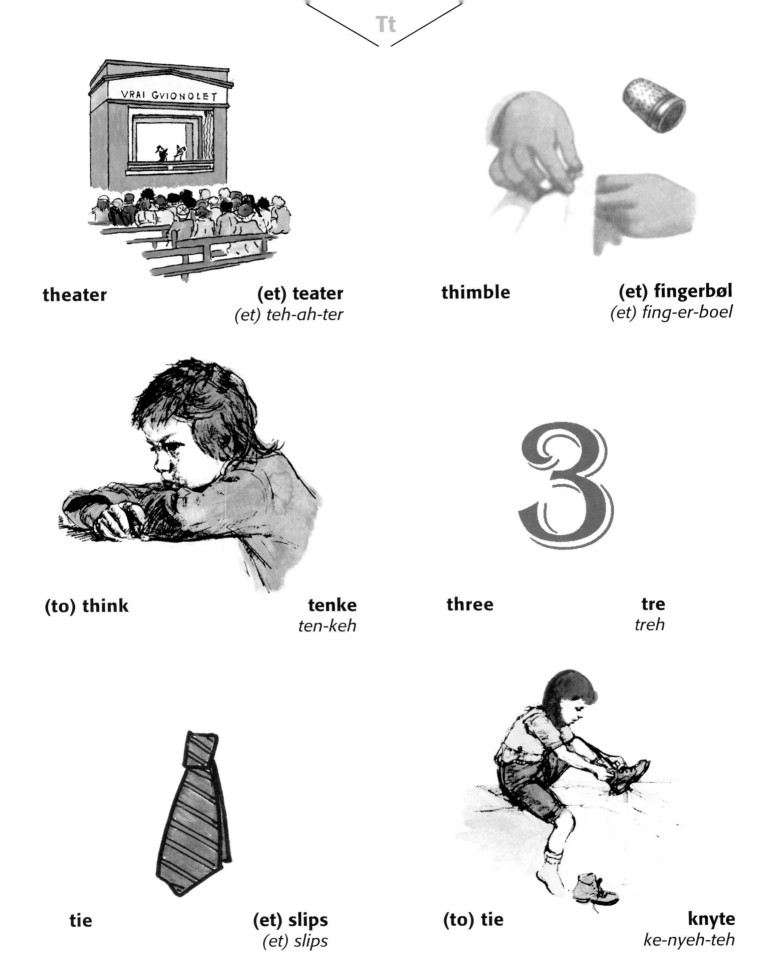

**theater**     **(et) teater**
*(et) teh-ah-ter*

**thimble**     **(et) fingerbøl**
*(et) fing-er-boel*

**(to) think**     **tenke**
*ten-keh*

**three**     **tre**
*treh*

**tie**     **(et) slips**
*(et) slips*

**(to) tie**     **knyte**
*ke-nyeh-teh*

**tiger**     **(en) tiger**
*(ehn) tee-ger*

**toaster**     **(en) brødrister**
*(ehn) broe-rist-er*

**tomato**     **(en) tomat**
*(ehn) to-maht*

**toucan**     **(en) tukan**
*(ehn) tuh-kahn*

**towel**     **(et) håndkle**
*(et) hohn-kleh*

**tower**     **(et) tårn**
*(et) tohrn*

**toy box**     **(en) leketøykasse**
*(ehn) leh-keh-toei-kahs-eh*

**tracks**     **spor**
*spoor*

**train station**     **(en) jernbanestasjon**
*(ehn) yayrn-bah-neh-stah-shohn*

**tray**     **(et) brett**
*(et) breht*

**tree**     **(et) tre**
*(et) treh*

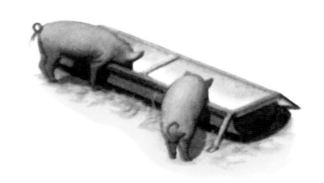

**trough**     **(en) grisetro**
*(ehn) gree-she-troo*

**truck**

**(en) lastebil**
*(ehn) lust-eh-beel*

**trumpet**     **(en) trompet**
*(ehn) trom-peht*

**tulip**     **(en) tulipan**
*(ehn) tuh-lee-pahn*

**tunnel**     **(en) tunnel**
*(ehn) tuh-nehl*

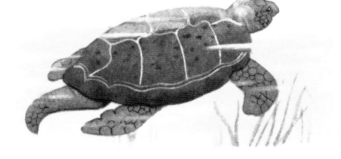

**turtle**     **(en/ei) skilpadde**
*(ehn/ey) shil-pahd-deh*

**twins**     **tvillinger**
*tvill-ing-er*

**two**     **to**
*too*

**umbrella**     **(en) paraply**
*(ehn) par-ah-plyeh*

**uphill**     **oppoverbakke**
*op-oh-ver-buk-keh*

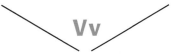

Vv

**vase**     **(en) vase**
*(ehn) vahs-eh*

**veil**     **(et) slør**
*(et) sloer*

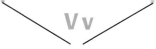

**village**

**(en) by**
*(ehn) byeh*

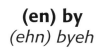

**violet**

**(en) fiol**
*(ehn) fee-ool*

**violin**

**(en) fiolin**
*(ehn) fee-ool-een*

**voyage**

**(en) reise**
*(ehn) rey-seh*

**waiter**　　　　**(en) kelner**
*(ehn) kel-ner*

**(to) wake up**　　　　**våkne**
*voh-kneh*

**walrus**　　　　**(en) hvalross**
*(ehn) vahl-rohss*

**(to) wash**　　　　**vaske seg**
*vah-skeh sey*

**watch**　　　　**(en/ei) klokke**
*(ehn/ey) klohk-keh*

**(to) watch**　　　　**se på**
*she poh*

**(to) water**       **vanne**
*vahn-neh*

**waterfall**       **(en) foss**
*(ehn) fohss*

**watering can**       **(en) hagesprøyte**
*(ehn) hah-geh-sproeyeh-teh*

**watermelon**       **(en) vannmelon**
*(ehn) vahnn-meh-loon*

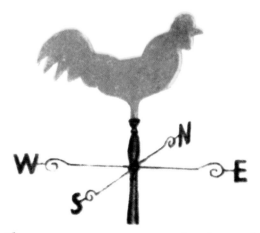

**weather vane**       **(en) værhane**
*(ehn) vayr-hahn-eh*

**(to) weigh**       **veie**
*vey-eh*

**whale**      **(en) hval**
*(ehn) vahl*

**wheel**      **(et) hjul**
*(et) yuhl*

**wheelbarrow**      **(en) trillebår**
*(ehn) trill-eh-bohr*

**whiskers**      **(et) værhår**
*(et) vayr-hohr*

**(to) whisper**      **hviske**
*visk-eh*

**whistle**      **(en) fløyte**
*(ehn) floeyeh-teh*

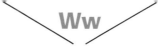

**white** **hvit**
*veet*

**wig** **(en) parykk**
*(ehn) pah-ryehk*

**wind** **(en) vind**
*(ehn) vihn*

**window** **(et) vindu**
*(et) vihn-duh*

**wings** **vinger**
*ving-er*

**winter** **(en) vinter**
*(ehn) vin-ter*

**wolf**

**(en) ulv**
*(ehn) uhlv*

**wood**

**(en) ved**
*(ehn) veh*

**word**

**(et) ord**
*(et) oor*

**(to) write**

**skrive**
*skree-veh*

**yellow**

**gul**
*guhl*

**zebra**

**(en) sebra**
*(ehn) seh-bra*

## A

| | |
|---|---|
| "Adjø" | "Good-bye" |
| agurk (en) | cucumber |
| akvarium (et) | aquarium |
| albue (en) | elbow |
| alfabet (et) | alphabet |
| alligator (en) | alligator |
| ananas (en) | pineapple |
| and (en) | duck |
| ansikt (et) | face |
| antilope (en) | antelope |
| apekatt (en) | monkey |
| appelsin (en) | orange |
| armbånd (et) | bracelet |
| avis (en) | newspaper |

## B

| | |
|---|---|
| baby (en) | baby |
| badestrand (en) | beach |
| bagasje | luggage |
| baker (en) | baker |
| ball (en) | ball |
| ballong (en) | balloon |
| banan (en) | banana |
| bein (et) | bone; leg |
| belte (et) | belt |
| benk (en) | bench |
| bestefar (en) | grandfather |
| bestemor (en/ei) | grandmother |
| bever (en) | beaver |
| bie (en) | bee |
| bil (en) | car |
| bille (en) | beetle |
| bjelle (en) | bell |
| bjørn (en) | bear |
| blad (et) | leaf |
| blomst (en) | flower |
| blyant (en) | pencil |
| blå | blue |
| bok (en) | book |
| bolle (en) | bowl |
| bord (et) | table |

| | |
|---|---|
| brannhydrant (en) | hydrant |
| bregne (en) | fern |
| brett (et) | tray |
| briller | glasses |
| bringebær (et) | raspberry |
| bro (en) | bridge |
| bror (en) | brother |
| brun | brown |
| brød (et) | bread |
| brødrister (en) | toaster |
| bue (en) | arch |
| by (en) | village |
| byggkorn (et) | barley |
| bære | (to) carry |
| børste (en) | brush |
| bål (et) | fire |
| båt (en) | boat |

## D

| | |
|---|---|
| danse | (to) dance |
| dato (en) | date |
| delfin (en) | dolphin |
| dra | (to) pull |
| drage (en) | dragon |
| drikke | (to) drink |
| drivhus (et) | greenhouse |
| dronning (en/ei) | queen |
| drosje (en) | cab |
| druer | grapes |
| due (en) | pigeon |
| dukke (en) | doll |
| dukkehus (et) | dollhouse |
| dumphuske (en) | seesaw |
| dusj (en) | shower |
| dyne (en/ei) | comforter |

## E

| | |
|---|---|
| edderkopp (en) | spider |
| egg (et) | egg |
| eggplante (en) | eggplant |
| ekorn (et) | squirrel |
| elefant (en) | elephant |
| elv (en) | river |
| en/ei/et | one |

| | |
|---|---|
| eple (et) | apple |
| esel (et) | donkey |
| eskimo (en) | Eskimo |

## F

| | |
|---|---|
| fallskjerm (en) | parachute |
| far (en) | father |
| farge (en) | paint (color) |
| feie | (to) sweep |
| fem | five |
| fersken (en) | peach |
| finger (en) | finger |
| fingerbøl (et) | thimble |
| fiol (en) | violet |
| fiolin (en) | violin |
| fire | four |
| fisk (en) | fish |
| fiske | (to) fish |
| fjell (et) | mountain |
| fjernsyn (et) | television |
| fjær (en) | feather |
| flagg (et) | flag |
| flaggermus (en) | bat |
| flaske (en) | bottle |
| fly (et) | airplane |
| fly | (to) fly |
| flyte | (to) float |
| fløyte (en) | whistle |
| folk (et) | people |
| foss (en) | waterfall |
| fot (en) | foot |
| fotografiapparat (et) | camera |
| frakk (en) | coat |
| frimerke (et) | stamp |
| frokost (en) | breakfast |
| frosk (en) | frog |
| frukt (en) | fruit |
| fruktblomst (en) | blossom |
| fugl (en) | bird |
| fuglebur (et) | birdcage |
| fuglerede (et) | nest |
| furutre (et) | pine |
| fyr (et) | lighthouse |

## G

| | |
|---|---|
| gaffel (en) | fork |
| gammel | old |
| gardin (en) | curtain |
| gaupe (en) | lynx |
| gave (en) | present |
| geit (en/ei) | goat |
| genser (en) | sweater |
| geranium (en) | geranium |
| gi | (to) give |
| gitar (en) | guitar |
| gjemme seg | (to) hide |
| gjerde (et) | fence |
| gjeter (en) | shepherd |
| glass (et) | glass |
| globus (en) | globe |
| "God natt" | "Good night" |
| grantre (et) | fir tree |
| grein (en) | branch |
| gresshoppe (en) | grasshopper |
| gresskar (et) | pumpkin |
| gressklipper (en | lawn mower |
| grevling (en) | badger |
| gris (en) | pig |
| grisetro (en) | trough |
| gryte (en/ei) | pot |
| grønn | green |
| gråte | (to) cry |
| gul | yellow |
| gullfisk (en) | goldfish |
| gulrot (en) | carrot |
| gummibåt (en) | raft |
| gutt (en) | boy |
| gå over (gata) | (to) cross (the street) |
| gås (en) | goose |

## H

| | |
|---|---|
| hage (en) | garden |
| hagesprøte (en) | watering can |
| hai (en) | shark |

| | |
|---|---|
| hakke | (to) peck |
| halsbånd (et) | necklace |
| hammer (en) | hammer |
| hamster (et) | hamster |
| hane (en) | rooster |
| hanske (en) | glove |
| hatt (en) | hat |
| hengekøye (en) | hammock |
| hengelås (en) | padlock |
| hest (en) | horse |
| hestesko (en) | horseshoe |
| hjerte (et) | heart |
| hjul (et) | wheel |
| hodeplagg (et) | headdress |
| honning (en) | honey |
| hoppe | (to) jump |
| horn | antlers; horns |
| hovedvei (en) | highway |
| hule (en) | cave |
| humle (en) | bumblebee |
| hummer (en) | lobster |
| hund (en) | dog |
| hundehus (et) | doghouse |
| hus (et) | house |
| huske (en) | swing |
| hval (en) | whale |
| hvalross (en) | walrus |
| hviske | whisper |
| hvit | white |
| høne (en/ei) | hen |
| høst (en) | autumn |
| høy (et) | hay |
| hånd (en) | hand |
| håndkle (et) | towel |
| håndveske (en) | handbag |

## I

| | |
|---|---|
| innhøsting (en) | harvest |
| instrument (et) | instrument |
| iris (en) | iris |
| isbit (en) | ice cubes |
| isbjørn (en) | polar bear |
| iskrem (en) | ice cream |

## J

| | |
|---|---|
| jakke (en) | jacket |
| jente (en/ei) | girl |
| jernbanestasjon (en) | train station |
| jockey (en) | jockey |
| jordbær (et) | strawberry |
| jorde (et) | field |
| juletre (et) | Christmas tree |

## K

| | |
|---|---|
| kafé (en) | café |
| kake (en) | cake |
| kaktus (en) | cactus |
| kam (en) | comb |
| kamel (en) | camel |
| kanin (en) | rabbit |
| kano (en) | canoe |
| kaptein (en) | captain |
| kart (et) | map |
| katt (en) | cat |
| kattunge (en) | kitten |
| kelner (en) | waiter |
| kenguru (en) | kangaroo |
| kikkert (en) | binoculars |
| kirsebær (et) | cherry |
| kjeks (en) | cracker |
| kjelke (en) | sled |
| kjerne (en) | pit |
| kjole (en) | dress |
| kjøleskap (et) | refrigerator |
| klatre | (to) climb |
| klemme | (to) hug |
| klokke (en/ei) | watch |
| klosser | blocks |
| klovn (en) | clown |
| knappenål (en/ei) | pin |
| kniv (en) | knife |
| knute (en) | knot |
| knyte | (to) tie |
| knyttneve (en) | fist |

**koalabjørn (en)** koala bear
**kokosnøtt (en)** coconut
**komfyr (en)** stove
**kompass (et)** compass
**konvolutt (en)** envelope
**kork (en)** cork
**kort (et)** card
**kost (en)** broom
**krabbe** (to) crawl
**krone (en)** crown
**ku (en/ei)** cow
**kurv (en)** basket
**kålhode (et)** cabbage

## L

**lage mat** (to) cook
**lam (et)** lamb
**lampe (en)** lamp
**lapp (en)** patch
**lastebil (en)** truck
**latter (en)** laughter
**lavendel (en)** lavender
**leke** (to) play
**leketøykasse (en)** toy box
**lese** (to) read
**linjal (en)** ruler
**liten** small
**lokomotiv (et)** engine
**lommelykt (en)** flashlight
**lommetørkle (et)** handkerchief
**lue (en/ei)** cap
**lunsj (en)** lunch
**lys (et)** candle
**lyspære (en)** lightbulb
**lytte** (to) listen
**løk (en)** onion
**lønneblad (et)** maple leaf
**løpe** (to) run
**løve (en)** lion
**løvetann (en)** dandelion
**lås (en)** lock

## M

**magnet (en)** magnet
**maiskolbe (en)** corn
**maler (en)** painter

**marihøne (en/ei)** ladybug
**markmus (en/ei)** field mouse
**maske (en)** mask
**mate** (to) feed
**melkemann (en)** milkman
**mor (en/ei)** mother
**mugge (en)** pitcher
**munn (en)** mouth
**mus (en/ei)** mouse
**musikk (en)** music
**møbler** furniture
**måke (en)** seagull
**måne (en)** moon

## N

**naken** naked
**nattergal (en)** nightingale
**nebbdyr (et)** platypus
**nesehorn (et)** rhinoceros
**ni** nine
**notisbok (en)** notebook
**nummer (et)** number
**nøkkel (en)** key
**nøtt (en/ei)** nut
**nål (en/ei)** needle

## O

**okse (en)** ox
**oppoverbakke** uphill
**oppslagstavle (en)** bulletin board
**ord (et)** word
**ost (en)** cheese

## P

**pai (en)** pie
**palmetre (et)** palm tree
**papegøye (en)** parrot
**papir (et)** paper
**paraply (en)** umbrella
**park (en)** park
**parykk (en)** wig
**pass (et)** passport
**passasjerbåt (en)** ocean liner
**pelikan (en)** pelican
**penger** money

**piano (et)** piano
**pil (en)** arrow
**pingvin (en)** penguin
**pinnsvin (et)** hedgehog
**pipe (en/ei)** chimney
**plomme (en)** plum
**plukke** (to) gather
**ponni (en)** pony
**port (en)** gate
**potet (en)** potato
**pyjamas (en)** pajamas
**pult (en)** desk
**puslespill (et)** jigsaw puzzle
**pute (en/ei)** pillow
**pære (en)** pear

## R

**radio (en)** radio
**rakett (en)** rocket
**ramme (en)** frame
**reddik (en)** radish
**redsel (en)** fear
**regn (et)** rain
**regnbue (en)** rainbow
**regnfrakk (en)** raincoat
**reise (en)** voyage
**rev (en)** fox
**ridder (en)** knight
**ring (en)** ring
**ringe** (to) ring
**ro** (to) row
**rose (en)** rose
**rot (en)** root
**rotete** messy
**rulletrapp (en)** escalator

ryggsekk (en) backpack
rød red
rådyr (et) deer

# S

salathode (et) lettuce
saks (en) scissors
salt (et) salt
sau (en) sheep
se på (to) watch
sebra (en) zebra
seile (to) sail
seks six
seng (en/ei) bed
sikkerhetsnål (en/ei) safety pin
sil (en) sieve
sirkus (et) circus
sitron (en) lemon
sitte (to) sit
sjiraff (en) giraffe
sjokolade (en) chocolate
sjonglør (en) juggler
sju seven
sjuk sick
sjømann (en) sailor
sjøstjerne (en) starfish
skillpadde (en/ei) turtle
skip (et) ship
skitten dirty
skjell (et) shell
skje (en) spoon
skjenke (to) pour
skjerf (et) scarf
skjorte (en) shirt
sko (en) shoe
skole (en) school
skrelle (to) peel
skrive (to) write
skrujern (et) screwdriver
sky (en) cloud
skøyteløp (et) ice-skating
slange (en) snake
slikke i seg (to) lap
slips (et) tie
slott (et) castle

slør (et) veil
smil (et) smile
småstein (en) pebble
snegle (en) snail
snø (en) snow
sofa (en) sofa
sommerfugl (en) butterfly
sopp (en) mushroom
sol (en/ei) sun
solsikke (en) sunflower
sove (to) sleep
spade (en) shovel
spann (et) bucket
speil (et) mirror
spindelvev (en) spiderweb
spise (to) eat
spor tracks
springvann (et) fountain
spurv (en) sparrow
sti (en) path
stige (en) ladder
stol (en) chair
stork (en) stork
strikke (to) knit
struts (en) ostrich
strykejern (et) iron
strømpe (en) sock
støvel (en) boot
sukkerbit (en) sugar cube
sukkertøy (et) candy

svart black
sy (to) sew
sykkel (en) bicycle
sylteagurk (en) pickle
syltetøy (et) jam
synge (to) sing
syren (en) lilac

# T

tak (et) roof
tallerken (en) plate
tau (et) rope
teater (et) theater
tegne (to) draw
tekanne (en) teapot
teddybjørn (en) teddy bear
telt (et) tent
tenke (to) think
tennisracket (en) racket
teppe (et) carpet
ti ten
tiger (en) tiger
timeglass (et) hourglass
to two
tom empty
tomat (en) tomato
torg (et) marketplace
trapp (en) stairs
tre three
tre (et) tree
trillebår (en) wheelbarrow
tromme (en) drum
trompet (en) trumpet
tryllekunstner (en) magician
tukan (en) toucan
tulipan (en) tulip
tunnel (en) tunnel
tunnelbane (en) subway
turteldue (en) lovebird
tvillinger twins
tømmerhogger (en) lumberjack
tønne (en) barrel

| | |
|---|---|
| **tårn (et)** | tower |

## U

| | |
|---|---|
| **ugle (en)** | owl |
| **ukeblad (et)** | magazine |
| **ulv (en)** | wolf |
| **utforske** | (to) explore |

## V

| | |
|---|---|
| **valp (en)** | puppy |
| **vanne** | (to) water |
| **vannmelon (en)** | watermelon |
| **vase (en)** | vase |
| **vaske seg** | (to) wash |
| **vaskebjørn (en)** | raccoon |
| **ved (en)** | wood |
| **vei (en)** | road |
| **veie** | (to) weigh |
| **venn (en)** | friend |
| **vifte (en)** | fan |
| **vind (en)** | wind |
| **vindu (et)** | window |
| **vindusskodde (en)** | shutter |
| **vinger** | wings |
| **vinter (en)** | winter |
| **vise** | (to) show |
| **vogn (en)** | coach |
| **vott (en)** | mitten |
| **vugge (en)** | cradle |
| **værhane (en)** | weather vane |
| **værhår (et)** | whiskers |
| **våkne** | (to) wake up |

## Ø

| | |
|---|---|
| **ørken (en)** | desert |
| **ørn (en)** | eagle |
| **øy (en/ei)** | island |
| **øye (et)** | eye |
| **øyenstikker (en)** | dragonfly |

## Å

| | |
|---|---|
| **åpen** | open |
| **åre (en/ei)** | oar |
| **åtte** | eight |

**Folk Tales from Bohemia**
Adolf Wenig
This folk tale collection is one of a kind, focusing uniquely on humankind's struggle with evil in the world. Delicately ornate red and black text and illustrations set the mood.
*Ages 9 and up*
90 pages • red and black illustrations • 5 1/2 x 8 1/4 • 0-7818-0718-2 • W • $14.95hc • (786)

**Czech, Moravian and Slovak Fairy Tales**
Parker Fillmore
Fifteen different classic, regional folk tales and 23 charming illustrations whisk the reader to places of romance, deception, royalty, and magic.
*Ages 12 and up*
243 pages • 23 b/w illustrations • 5 1/2 x 8 1/4 • 0-7818-0714-X • W • $14.95 hc • (792)

**Glass Mountain: Twenty-Eight Ancient Polish Folk Tales and Fables**
W.S. Kuniczak
Illustrated by Pat Bargielski
As a child in a far-away misty corner of Volhynia, W.S. Kuniczak was carried away to an extraordinary world of magic and illusion by the folk tales of his Polish nurse.
171 pages • 6 x 9 • 8 illustrations • 0-7818-0552-X • W • $16.95hc • (645)

**Old Polish Legends**
Retold by F.C. Anstruther
Wood engravings by J. Sekalski
This fine collection of eleven fairy tales, with an introduction by Zymunt Nowakowski, was first published in Scotland during World War II.
66 pages • 7 1/4 x 9 • 11 woodcut engravings • 0-7818-0521-X • W • $11.95hc • (653)

**Folk Tales from Russia**
by Donald A. Mackenzie
With nearly 200 pages and 8 full-page black-and-white illustrations, the reader will be charmed by these legendary folk tales that symbolically weave magical fantasy with the historic events of Russia's past.
*Ages 12 and up*
192 pages • 8 b/w illustrations • 5 1/2 x 8 1/4 • 0-7818-0696-8 • W • $12.50hc • (788)

**Fairy Gold: A Book of Classic English Fairy Tales**
Chosen by Ernest Rhys
Illustrated by Herbert Cole
Forty-nine imaginative black and white illustrations accompany thirty classic tales, including such beloved stories as "Jack and the Bean Stalk" and "The Three Bears."
*Ages 12 and up*
236 pages • 5 1/2 x 8 1/4 • 49 b/w illustrations • 0-7818-0700-X • W • $14.95hc • (790)

### Tales of Languedoc: From the South of France
Samuel Jacques Brun
For readers of all ages, here is a masterful collection of folk tales from the south of France.
*Ages 12 and up*
248 pages • 33 b/w sketches • 5 1/2 x 8 1/4 • 0-7818-0715-8 • W • $14.95hc • (793)

### Twenty Scottish Tales and Legends
Edited by Cyril Swinson
Illustrated by Allan Stewart
Twenty enchanting stories take the reader to an extraordinary world of magic harps, angry giants, mysterious spells and gallant Knights.
*Ages 9 and up*
215 pages • 5 1/2 x 8 1/4 • 8 b/w illustrations • 0-7818-0701-8 • W • $14.95 hc • (789)

### Swedish Fairy Tales
Translated by H. L. Braekstad
A unique blending of enchantment, adventure, comedy, and romance make this collection of Swedish fairy tales a must-have for any library.
*Ages 9 and up*
190 pages • 21 b/w illustrations • 51/2 x 81/4 • 0-7818-0717-4 • W • $12.50hc • (787)

### The Little Mermaid and Other Tales
Hans Christian Andersen
Here is a near replica of the first American edition of 27 classic fairy tales from the masterful Hans Christian Andersen.
*Ages 9 and up*
508 pages • b/w illustrations • 6 x 9 • 0-7818-0720-4 • W • $19.95hc • (791)

### Pakistani Folk Tales: Toontoony Pie and Other Stories
Ashraf Siddiqui and Marilyn Lerch
Illustrated by Jan Fairservis
In these 22 folk tales are found not only the familiar figures of folklore—kings and beautiful princesses—but the magic of the Far East, cunning jackals, and wise holy men.
*Ages 7 and up*
158 pages • 6 1/2 x 8 1/2 • 38 illustrations • 0-7818-0703-4 • W • $12.50hc • (784)

### Folk Tales from Chile
Brenda Hughes
This selection of 15 tales gives a taste of the variety of Chile's rich folklore. Fifteen charming illustrations accompany the text.
*Ages 7 and up*
121 pages • 5 1/2 x 8 1/4 • 15 illustrations • 0-7818-0712-3 • W • $12.50hc • (785)

All prices subject to change. **To purchase Hippocrene Books** contact your local bookstore, call (718) 454-2366, or write to: HIPPOCRENE BOOKS, 171 Madison Avenue, New York, NY 10016. Please enclose check or money order, adding $5.00 shipping (UPS) for the first book and $.50 for each additional book.